TOP YOUTUBE STARS™

SHANE DAWSON

Actor and Author with More than **4 BILLION VIEWS**

KERRY HINTON

rosen publishing's
rosen
central®

New York

Library of Congress Cataloging-in-Publication Data

Names: Hinton, Kerry, author.
Title: Shane Dawson / Kerry Hinton.
Description: First edition. | New York : Rosen Central, 2020. | Series: Top YouTube stars | Includes bibliographical references and index.
Identifiers: LCCN 2018049123| ISBN 9781725346161 (library bound) | ISBN 9781725346154 (pbk.)
Subjects: LCSH: Dawson, Shane, 1988– —Juvenile literature. | Comedians—United States—Biography—Juvenile literature. | Actors—United States—Biography—Juvenile literature. | Internet personalities—United States—Biography—Juvenile literature. | YouTube (Electronic resource)—Biography—Juvenile literature.
Classification: LCC PN2287.D39 H57 2019 | DDC 792.702/8092 [B]—dc23
LC record available at https://lccn.loc.gov/2018049123

Manufactured in the United States of America

On the cover: YouTube personality Shane Dawson arrives at the 2014 Los Angeles premiere of the Starz film *Not Cool*, which he produced, directed, and edited.

CONTENTS

INTRODUCTION

On April 24, 2005, a nineteen-second video called *Me at the Zoo* was uploaded to YouTube, a new website that had been founded just two months earlier. It features Yakov Lavitsky, a friend of Jawed Karim (one of the site's founders), filming himself in front of elephants at the San Diego Zoo. This simple video would go on to change the internet forever. Today, more than 1.8 billion people visit YouTube every day—second only to Facebook. YouTube's worldwide popularity has led millions of fans to search for content on the site.

On YouTube, popularity can actually provide a career for some stars if their videos gain enough views. What type of video draws the biggest crowds? The answer to the question of what to watch is different for everyone. Some look for well-known celebrities. Some like to watch video game replays and live events. Others seek out beauty tips. No matter what the focus may be, many types of videos draw millions of viewers. If a person is fortunate enough and talented enough, he or she can rise to the top of the YouTuber game. There is something for everyone on YouTube, but some of the biggest stars draw millions of viewers who want to see everyday people simply be themselves. These are today's YouTube stars. One of the first people to gain this kind of online stardom was Shane Dawson.

Shane Dawson has been one of the best-known YouTube stars for over ten years. Among other things, he is a comedian, author, writer, actor, director, and singer. Dawson first became famous for his comedic talents. In 2008, Dawson began making a series of sketch videos, playing a variety of comic characters, including Shanay-nay, Ned the Nerd, S. Deezy, and Shane's Mom. Millions have watched Dawson's videos since then, and today he

4

has more than seventeen million YouTube subscribers; and his videos have been viewed more than four billion times. In addition to YouTube, Dawson has millions of followers on Facebook, Instagram, and Twitter.

Dawson's down-to-earth manner and conversational tone are two of his strongest qualities. His fans subscribe to his YouTube channels to hear about his struggles as well as laugh at his jokes. The hard times he has gone through make him even more real and accessible to his subscribers. The keys to understanding Dawson and his work today are contained in his past. Long before he became internationally known, Dawson was not very different from his average fan: a normal teen trying to fit in and figure out life.

Shane Dawson's multiple talents have allowed him to maintain his place as one of YouTube's most popular stars for more than ten years.

CHAPTER ONE

A Star Is Born

Before he became a global YouTube celebrity, Shane Dawson was just a normal kid living in Southern California. Like many of his fans, Dawson dealt with a less than perfect childhood. The trials and setbacks that Dawson experienced through his teens have made him extremely relatable to his fans. Subscribers love Dawson because they feel they are just like him, flaws and mistakes included.

A ROUGH CHILDHOOD

Shane Lee Yaw was born in Long Beach, California, on July 19, 1988. As a child, he faced many challenges that have affected him and his art to this day. Dawson's father was an alcoholic and was verbally abusive to Dawson and his brothers. When he was nine years old, Dawson's parents divorced and his father moved out of the family home. Dawson and his two brothers, Jacob and Jared, were left to live with their mother in a single-parent household.

Dawson was an overweight child. By the time he was seven, he weighed close to 200 pounds (91 kilograms). During his teen years, Dawson described himself as "morbidly obese."

Long Beach, California, is fewer than 20 miles (32 kilometers) from Los Angeles. Because of its location and scenic beauty, it's popular for television and movie shoots.

He reached a maximum weight of 330 pounds (150 kg) as a teenager. Dawson was often shamed and bullied because of his weight, which he has discussed in some of his blog posts and videos. Dawson's weight issues led to low self-esteem and depression. As a result, he didn't engage much with other kids at school. Since much of his social and school life was difficult, Dawson escaped these problems by spending more time at home. Creativity was Dawson's main source of comfort while he was growing up. He began making comedy videos at home when he was seven years old, often with his brother Jared (known on YouTube as CoolGuyWithGlasses).

SHANE YAW, MEET SHANE DAWSON

Fans have different theories about why Dawson changed his last name from Yaw to Dawson. Some believe he changed it to distance himself from his father and traumatic childhood. Actually, Dawson's agent suggested the name change to give Dawson's online persona a catchier last name. The choice of Dawson's stage name has also intrigued fans. A segment of Dawson's followers point to Jack Dawson, a character played by Leonardo DiCaprio in the 1997 film *Titanic*. However, during a question and answer session with BlogTV in 2009, Shane revealed that his stage name comes from both his love for *Titanic* and his affection for *Dawson's Creek*, a television show from the late 1990s.

SHANE'S FIRST VIDEOS

Dawson continued to battle his weight throughout high school. As he prepared for his graduation from Lakewood High School, he realized that his gown for the ceremony was much too small. He solved the problem by sewing two gowns together, but was so bothered by the experience that he fully committed himself to losing weight and getting healthier. After trying to lose weight with Weight Watchers more than ten times, Dawson looked for other solutions. He signed up with a nutrition company called Jenny Craig in 2006. This change worked—Dawson lost 150 pounds (68 kg) in nine months. Today, he keeps his weight under control by working out regularly—he ends some videos by telling his fans he is on his way to the gym.

After his radical transformation, Dawson began working for the company that had helped him change his body and outlook on life. Jenny Craig also employed Dawson's mother and one of his brothers. During this time, Dawson continued to make videos and turned in some of them as homework. His first video was an assignment about dictatorships for a college Economics class. Many of these early videos have been deleted from YouTube. He also began to think about a career as an actor and director. He decided that YouTube would be a perfect place to upload and store his growing catalog. In March 2008, he created Shane Dawson TV, the first of three YouTube channels he would upload to over the next ten years. In "The 411," Dawson's first video, he addresses the audience by saying "What's cracking, YouTubers?" and states his mission: to make and share a video blog about everything in his life, from the large to the small. Dawson continued to post these vlogs over the next few months.

A LITTLE BIT OF FAME

In June 2008, Dawson uploaded a video that was very different from anything he had filmed before. "Hodini's Street Magic" was a comedy sketch that Dawson wrote and directed. In the video, Dawson appears in a pink wig as Hodini, a sassy magician performing tricks for and on random people on the street. The video introduced fans to some themes that Dawson would use throughout his career: wigs, dressing in drag, and some foul language. At the end of the video, Dawson addresses his fans, asking them not to tell him if they don't like his video because an unsuccessful video would force him to work at Jenny Craig Weight Loss Center and abandon his dreams.

While at Jenny Craig, Dawson's home and work lives began to mix. That summer, he uploaded a video he shot at work called

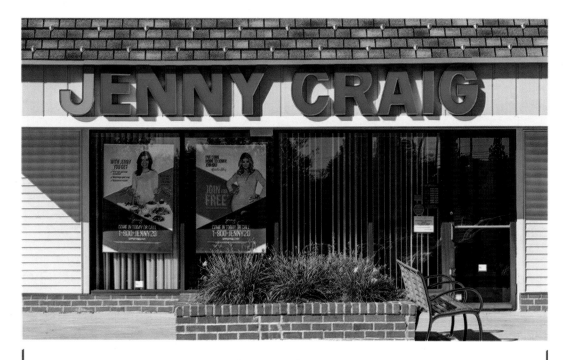

Shane Dawson used the Long Beach Jenny Craig Weight Loss Center as a makeshift studio for filming some of his earliest YouTube videos.

"Days of My Life." When his employers discovered this, Dawson was fired; unfortunately, Jenny Craig also fired his mother and brother as well as some other employees. The video was deleted from YouTube and did not reappear for three years. In the vlog "YOUTUBE GOT ME FIRED," Dawson reveals that Jenny Craig wanted to sue him for his unauthorized video. This was a dark time for Dawson, but the experience taught him to stay positive. He later realized that things could have been worse and decided to keep following his dreams.

Dawson soon found work as a security guard at a local aquarium and continued to make and upload videos in his off time. As his catalog grew, so did his number of viewers. When Dawson's videos reached fifty thousand views, YouTube accepted him into their brand-new Partner Program. After that, Dawson began to earn money when viewers clicked on advertisements attached to his videos. Making a living on YouTube began to look like a real possibility for Dawson. In an interview with Tom Ward of *Forbes*, Dawson admitted later that he wasn't making as much money as he could have because much of his content was raunchy and inappropriate for younger viewers. Dawson used his new earnings to move his mother and brother from Long Beach to Los Angeles.

DAWSON GOES VIRAL

On September 12, 2008, Dawson uploaded "Fred Is Dead!" In the video, Dawson plays two roles. The first is Fred Figglehorn—a character created and played by fellow YouTuber Lucas Cruikshank. In the original videos, Fred is a six-year-old boy with a high, whiny voice who gets angry very easily. At the time, Cruikshank had the most subscribers on YouTube. In "Fred Is Dead!" Dawson tells viewers that he has kidnapped Fred and has a plan to kill him in order to have more subscribers. "Fred Is Dead!" also features the first appearance of Dawson's female character Shanaynay. Shanaynay is an ex-convict who uses foul language, takes drugs, and is extremely rude. In the video, she tells Fred that Dawson has hired her to kill him. "Fred Is Dead!" may seem dark at first, but the mood lightens when Shanaynay realizes Fred cannot be killed. The video went viral. Hundreds of thousands of people watched and rewatched it, giving Dawson his real first taste of YouTube stardom. As of November 2018, "Fred Is Dead!" has been viewed more than twenty-five million times. Dawson had announced his arrival, and millions of young people showed their approval.

CHAPTER TWO

2008 to 2010: "Hey, What's Up, You Guys?"

Although many of Dawson's first videos were meant to be gross, outrageous, and funny, many of them also offer inspiration to his fans. In "Flaws" (2008) he says: "I don't care who you are, everybody has flaws. Even the Jonas Brothers." The video then shows clips of other YouTubers sharing their personal flaws. This combination of humor and honesty appealed to his subscribers, and Dawson's fan base continued to grow.

MORE OUTPUT

Part of what made Dawson's video "Fred Is Dead" go viral was its subject. By making a funny sketch imitating a character created by the world's most famous YouTuber, Dawson drew a new group of fans to him. This happens frequently, but in Dawson's case, many of the new viewers subscribed to Shane Dawson TV. Fortunately, Dawson had much more to show his audience and continued to make new and more adventurous videos using costumes, wigs, and accents. Dawson still revealed personal details to his audience, but also attempted different types of videos.

He was trying out a new video style when he made "Sarah Palin Music Video," which featured an original song in which Dawson was dressed up as the 2008 vice presidential candidate. In later years, Dawson would parody other popular artists, including Shania Twain, Miley Cyrus, and Lady Gaga. Some sketches were devoted to reviews and criticisms of *Twilight* and other popular movies. Dawson uploaded twice the number of videos in 2009 than he did in 2008. Although Dawson developed new characters, some of his more popular characters made repeat appearances. For example, Shanaynay appeared in more than a dozen videos between 2008 and 2011.

Dawson's early amateur videos eventually landed him the opportunity to write and direct for major cable networks. Here he appears at the 2014 premiere of the television series *Outlander*.

MORE CHANNELS

Over his career, Dawson has used three separate channels to connect with his

SKETCH COMEDY

Sketch comedy has existed since people have been performing for audiences. A sketch is a short written scene that normally lasts for anywhere from one to ten minutes. Some scenes are longer, but comedy sketches are meant to be short. Sketches are not single jokes; they explore a character or an issue through comedy. Sketches can take many forms and can be performed by one person or a group of many people. The first comedic sketches were performed for live audiences as early as the eighteenth century. Eventually, artists performed sketches on the radio, television, and finally on the internet. *Saturday Night Live*, *Sesame Street*, and *Robot Chicken* are all examples of shows that use comedy sketches. *MadTV*, a television sketch show that ran from 1995 to 2015, was Dawson's greatest inspiration. *MadTV* could often be shocking, offensive and ridiculous. This style of comedy had a huge influence on Dawson and can be seen in many of the videos he uploaded in the first ten years of his career.

The roots of Dawson's love for boundary-pushing comedy can be found in sketch-comedy television shows, such as *Saturday Night Live* and *MadTV*.

fans. As he became more famous, Dawson decided he needed more ways to present all of his different uploads. In 2009, he created two more YouTube channels. Each had a separate focus. ShaneDawsonTV2 was launched in April and featured behind the scenes vlogs of his video shoots. The channel also allowed Dawson and his fans to interact with each other. In the video series *Ask Shane*, Dawson answered questions from his fans. One of Dawson's other series, *Viewer Orgy Party*, did the opposite, with Dawson posing questions to his subscribers. In April 2015, Dawson renamed the channel HumanEmoji.

That same year, Dawson created shane, his third channel. As time went on, this became Dawson's only active channel. The other two channels are no longer in use today. The most recent HumanEmoji video was uploaded in 2012, and Shane Dawson TV has been inactive since December 2016. Today, shane is Dawson's primary channel and is used for all of his vlogs and original videos. As of November 2018, it had more than nineteen million subscribers.

WORKING TOGETHER

Dawson has been working with other YouTube stars almost as long as he has been uploading content. Over the years, he has worked with friends such as Joey Graceffa, Tyler Oakley, Miranda Sings, and iJustine. In 2009 he became a member of The Station, a YouTube sketch comedy channel created by actress and comedian LisaNova. The members included Sxephil, WhatadayDerek, and DaveDays. The first video, "ZOMBIES TAKE OVER YOUTUBE!!!!!!," went viral, but the channel lost popularity when it stopped posting videos on schedule. The Station's last official upload was in 2011.

YouTube celebrities (*from left*) Justine Ezarik, Dawson, and Joey Graceffa, shown here at the 2015 BookCon in New York City, often create work outside of YouTube, including scripts and books.

A YEAR TO REMEMBER

Dawson reached even greater heights in 2010, which also marked the five-year anniversary of YouTube. In just two years, Shane Dawson TV and ShaneDawsonTV2 had become two of the top ten most-subscribed YouTube channels. Even people outside of the world of YouTube began to notice Dawson and his popularity. In April, the *New York Times* published an article by Austin Considine about Dawson that mentioned his "potty mouth" and offensive comedy. David Ewalt of *Forbes* magazine named him the twenty-fifth-most-famous web celebrity of the year, saying: "A kid with a webcam can become a movie star." Dawson also won Choice Web Star at the 2010 Teen Choice Awards and Best Vlogger at the 2010 Streamy Awards.

Dawson tried his hand at acting, too, appearing in the horror web series *BlackBox TV Presents* in 2010. That Halloween, Dawson created "Haunted House Party," a "choose your own adventure" video for fans that made fun of classic Halloween horror movies. Dawson finished the year by making a ten-minute Christmas video with the Fine Brothers, two extremely popular YouTube comedians and filmmakers. Dawson wrote, starred in, and edited the collaboration, entitled "Santa's Dead: A Christmas Love Story." In this twisted holiday video, Santa comes to Dawson's home after being stabbed by Shanaynay. "Santa's Dead" features bad behavior, violence, and gross jokes; in other words, it's classic Dawson. Dawson agreed. In an interview with Megan O'Neill of *AdWeek*, he said:

> My humor has always been inappropriate and unapologetic. My childhood was very rough and my family relied on me to make the bad situations funny. I think my audience relates to my humor because a lot of them are going through tough times and they know that I'm going to make them laugh and get them through it. Anyone who is offended by my videos should know that my raunchy jokes and inappropriate subject matters come from a place of love and not hate. For every person I offend with my videos I know that there are hundreds of thousands more that are being helped by them.

CHAPTER THREE

2011 to 2013: Keep on Rising

In 2011, Dawson became increasingly visible more places than just YouTube. He continued to collaborate with the Fine Brothers and other celebrities. He also started exploring television, music, and podcasting. Instead of focusing on one of these areas, Dawson experimented with all of them at the same time. Most of these projects would be shown or promoted on YouTube.

TELEVISION, FILM, AND MUSIC

Dawson had been working on an idea for a half-hour YouTube comedy about a high school teen since 2010. A television network liked the idea and developed it with Dawson. Hopes were high, but the project never materialized. The project was never officially cancelled, but it seems unlikely that it will ever be made. Dawson's next television project was even closer to his experiences—a comedy about a teen who works at a weight-loss center. The show was called *Losin' It*. Like his first attempt at making a television show, this untitled show has not made it to the small screen yet. Dawson still continued to work on the

Many YouTube celebrities can connect more personally with their fans and earn additional income through public appearances at conventions such as VidCon.

project as well as an idea for a television talk show. While writing and pitching television shows, Dawson kept making small appearances in other projects. In 2012, he was a voice guest on *The High Fructose Adventures of Annoying Orange* on the Cartoon Network.

Dawson was also making progress in his music. In 2012, he released "Superluv!" his first single. The track was very popular in the United Kingdom and Ireland and reached the top two hundred singles. Other singles followed, including "High School: The Rap" and "Maybe This Christmas." These singles did not have extreme chart success but were viewed millions of times by Dawson's subscribers. His love of parody songs continued. Taylor Swift became a favorite source of material—Dawson recorded

MAKING MONEY ON YOUTUBE

The career of a YouTube celebrity can be very lucrative. When viewers watch a video for more than thirty seconds or click an ad associated with it, posters can make money—the amount depends on views and subscriptions. PewDiePie, one of the most famous YouTubers of all time, has more than sixty-six million subscribers who tune in regularly to watch his video game commentaries. As a result, he makes around $12 million per year.

PewDiePie has used his YouTube celebrity to pursue other projects, including books and a clothing line.

The biggest celebrities can become millionaires, but this is not the norm. Becoming (and staying) a star on YouTube takes a combination of talent, timing, and luck. Most YouTubers earn around $1 to $2 for every one thousand views. YouTube celebrities can also make money by endorsing certain brands in their videos and selling their own t-shirts and merchandise. YouTubers who can pitch products in their videos are known as influencers. Today, many YouTubers have links to their products on their channels. Outside of YouTube, celebrities connect with their fans through Instagram, Twitter, and Facebook, which gives them additional opportunities to find more subscribers and followers.

four parodies of her songs between 2012 and 2014. He also took a comic look at Miley Cyrus's "Wrecking Ball."

A LITTLE ROMANCE

Dawson's personal life improved during this time. In 2011, he began dating Lisa Schwartz. Lisa was also a YouTube personality. She created her YouTube channel lisbug in 2007 and had more than one million subscribers when she and Dawson began dating. She also acted in the lead role in *My Profile Story*, a Fine Brothers movie from 2009. The couple appeared in each other's uploads, and millions of followers tuned in for the latest developments in Dawson and Schwartz's relationship.

Today, many YouTube celebrities like Dawson, shown here in 2013 with his then-girlfriend Lisa Schwartz, have become much better known to the general public, which has increased their fan base.

SHANE AND FRIENDS

In June 2013, Dawson created and launched *Shane and Friends,* his first podcast. The show was available on iTunes and on Soundcloud in June. *Shane and Friends* was funny, but it didn't feature song spoofs or comedy sketches. The show focused more on interviews with celebrities and gossip about

SO YOU WANT TO BE A YOUTUBER, PART ONE: THE BASICS

Just because only a small percentage of YouTubers become famous, that shouldn't prevent you from seeing how far your career can go. Before you start writing a hit movie, some first steps need to be taken.

Computer and Internet

You must have a computer with internet access in order to share videos on YouTube and social media. It should have a fast connection for smooth recording and streaming of videos.

Gmail

Since Google owns YouTube, a Google account is required to upload videos. Anyone over the age of thirteen can open an account. If you're under that age, a parent or other adult must open the account for you. Your Google account will give you access to Gmail and YouTube.

Start a YouTube Channel

YouTube makes it incredibly easy to start a channel. Once you're signed in, click on your profile picture in the upper right hand corner. One of the options there is "My channel." Click on it and now you're all set to upload your latest vlogs, songs, and short films.

popular culture. Dawson noted that the controversial radio host Howard Stern was the inspiration for the show. Like Stern, Dawson enjoys being himself, even if some of his material is considered offensive. Dawson's admiration of Stern even affected the design of the show's recording studio—it was designed to look almost exactly like Howard Stern's. As he mentioned in an interview with Tom Ward of *Forbes*, "I want to have weirdos in here, like he does."

Guests have included YouTube stars, singers, and comedians. Tyler Oakley, Joey Graceffa, Jamie Kennedy, and Perez Hilton have all made appearances. For the first two years of the podcast, Lauren Schnepper recorded twenty-six episodes with Dawson. She left the podcast during season two in 2014 and was replaced by Jessie Buttafuoco. After five seasons, *Shane and Friends* took a break from recording new episodes, but the show never officially ended.

CHAPTER FOUR

2014 to 2016: Branching Out

V ery few YouTube stars can maintain a ten-year career, but Dawson has always managed to keep both himself and his audience interested and entertained. The secret to his success? Change. Dawson refuses to be defined by any one of his talents. Over the years, he has gradually added different skills and subjects to his catalog. After more than five years at the top of YouTube, Dawson keeps proving that he's more than a one-note performer.

NOT COOL

In 2014, Dawson participated in a cable television reality competition called *The Chair*. The show followed Dawson and another director as they worked with a $1 million budget to shoot a film. Each director was required to use the same script and shoot in Pittsburgh, Pennsylvania. *The Chair* also showed viewers behind-the-scenes footage of the directors promoting and releasing their films. After screening their films for a test audience, Dawson's film was chosen, and he was awarded $250,000 to use for his next full-length film.

Although Dawson won his competition against Anna Martemucci at the end of *The Chair*, Martemucci has continued to act and direct.

This money allowed Dawson to achieve one of his greatest dreams: directing and starring in a feature film. He directed and played the lead role in *Not Cool*, a raunchy comedy filled with gross-out humor. Lisa Schwartz was a member of the cast, too. In the movie, Dawson's character, Scott, comes home from college at Thanksgiving to find out that his girlfriend is breaking up with him. Over the next few days, Scott and his friend Tori have a crazy weekend before they head back to school. The movie did not do well with critics or at the box office. On the movie review site Rotten Tomatoes, *Not Cool* received the very low rating of 14 percent; however, 75 percent of Dawson's fans loved his first movie.

THE APOLOGY

African American vloggers began to speak out against some of Dawson's videos. Many of them believed that some of Dawson's content was racist. To them, videos featuring Dawson in black-face imitating celebrities, including Randy Jackson and Wendy Wilson, were offensive. Screenshots of Dawson in costume began to circulate online. Vloggers also complained that Dawson had never been banned because of these videos.

Many of Dawson's fans rushed to support him. Some of them even threatened the people accusing Dawson, even though Dawson had always been very outspoken against bullying. Dawson deleted the offensive videos and addressed his subscribers in "My Apology (Blackface & Offensive Videos)." According to the video, Dawson had not even known what blackface was until a month before his videos were singled out. He called the videos "stupid and offensive" and pledged to do better for his fans. "I care too much about you to teach you things like that," Dawson says in the video.

Amid the controversy, Dawson still remained one with his fans. In the fall of 2014, Dawson discussed his struggles with body dysmorphic disorder. After his weight loss in 2008, Dawson admitted he still had trouble accepting what his body looked like. In "My Eating Disorder," he reveals that he's been going to therapy to work on the issue.

When Dawson's content has created controversy in the past, he has been very quick to address his fans on YouTube to explain and apologize.

SO YOU WANT TO BE A YOUTUBER, PART TWO: EQUIPMENT

After setting up accounts and your computer, the next step is to decide what sort of equipment you'll need to make your presence known. Some research is necessary before you buy. Equipment can range in price, so make sure you're not spending money on gear that may be too advanced for your needs. Getting advice is important. Many YouTube stars make videos that focus on the gear they use. Experts at your local electronics store can also help you make the best choice for your budget.

Camera

This is the most essential part of a video maker's toolbox. The types vary; video can be recorded using a cell phone, webcam, camcorder, or digital camera. If you can, choose a camera that can record in high definition—most YouTube stars record in 1080p. You'll also need a tripod or stand to hold your camera steady for the best result.

Lighting

Videos that are recorded indoors usually need some type of lighting besides a desk lamp or ceiling light. The better the lighting, the better the quality of the video you're recording. Many YouTube stars choose lighting that looks soft and natural. Different types of videos require their own special lighting.

Microphone

YouTubers want to be heard, and choosing the best microphone for your needs is important. Having sound that doesn't match video quality could cost you views and subscribers. Successful YouTube

(CONTINUED ON THE NEXT PAGE)

(*CONTINUED FROM THE PREVIOUS PAGE*)

personalities usually avoid using the microphones that are built into laptops or cameras.

Video Editing Software

After filming is finished, video editing software is used to add special effects and make the finished product look more professional. YouTube has a free video editor, but separate video editing software can offer more options for tricking out your upload with special effects.

MIND BLOWING CONSPIRACY THEORIES

Dawson kicked off 2015 with a new video series entitled *Mind Blowing Conspiracy Theories*. These videos have become some of Dawson's most viewed and subscribed posts. With titles like "SCARY CONSPIRACY VIDEOS!" and "CELEBRITY CONSPIRACY VIDEOS!" Dawson tackled many conspiracies and urban legends, such as what happened on 9/11, flat earth theories, and the idea that some celebrities may

Shane's two nonfiction books were a huge success with fans. They also received respect from media critics.

actually be reptiles. Dawson has made more than fifty of these fan favorite videos.

READER, MEET AUTHOR

Dawson published his first book in 2015. *I Hate Myselfie: A Collection of Essays* was exactly what his fans wanted. For them, the book was funny, conversational, and inspirational. In the essays, Dawson opens up even more than ever about his father, growing up poor, and being bullied. Each of the book's eighteen chapters features a fan drawing that represents the essay's subject. Dawson also lets his fans know that his online life is not always completely real. By sharing stories about his saddest and most embarrassing moments, Dawson fans saw more proof that Dawson was a regular person, too. The book reached number one on the *New York Times* bestseller list in its first two weeks in print.

COMING OUT

In July 2015, Dawson informed his subscribers that his relationship with Lisa Schwartz was over in his most personal video to date: "I'm Bisexual." Dawson explained that he wanted to date both men and women. He used his own public struggles to reassure his viewers. In the video, he says, "Love who you want to love. Life is short. Nobody's going to hate you for it." In 2016, Dawson announced on Instagram his relationship with Ryland Adams, the host of *Clevver News*, a celebrity and popular culture website with its own YouTube channel. Dawson examined the joys and struggles of coming out in his second book, *It Gets Worse: A Collection of Essays*. The book repeated the success of his first, hitting the *New York Times* bestseller list at number one.

CHAPTER FIVE

2017 to the Present: Growing Up

As Dawson and his fans grew older, their interests began to change. By 2017, Dawson's content was much more mature than his Shanaynay videos and *Not Cool*. Dawson began to think much more deeply about himself, his relationships with his family, and his responsibility to his fan base.

THE SHANE DAWSON INTERVIEWS

In late 2017, Dawson began to explore other types of video making. His videos from the early days up through *Mind Blowing Conspiracy Theories* were still a hit with fans, but Dawson felt the need to reflect on his life and the events that made him who he is. His first two documentaries were very personal. In "CONFRONTING MY FIRST LOVE," he reconnects with Blair, his first love. After five years without communicating, Dawson and Blair talk about their relationship. There are funny and serious moments as they confront their past history. This video got almost ten million views within a year.

The next video took a look at Dawson's relationship with his father. In "CONFRONTING MY DAD," Dawson asks his dad some difficult questions, including why he abandoned his family. Dawson's dad apologizes for not being around during Dawson's childhood and discusses other regrets he has. At the end of the video, Dawson's dad says, "I can't go back, but we can start forward, and I'm happy about that." Dawson and his dad hug and plan to meet more often.

RESPONDING TO THE CRITICS

In early 2018, a few old clips from *Shane and Friends* started to pop up around the internet. Although he considered not addressing this old material, he felt that he needed to. Dawson reminded people that he had not only apologized, but also

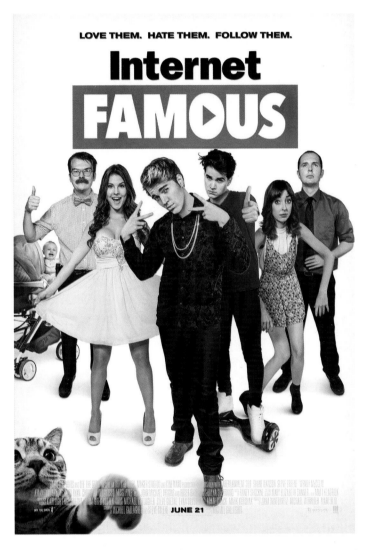

LOVE THEM. HATE THEM. FOLLOW THEM.

Internet FAMOUS

JUNE 21

The US poster of 2016's *Internet Famous* features (*from left*): Steve Green, Amanda Cerny, Shane Dawson, Christian Delgrosso, Wendy McColm, and Richard Ryan.

SO YOU WANT TO BE A YOUTUBER, PART THREE: STARDOM AWAITS

Now that you have internet access and proper equipment, it's time for the real work to begin. There are a lot of things to consider before you start filming your masterpiece, though.

Pick a Skill

Think about what skills you have. Can you give good advice or beauty tips? Do you want to show the world your video game skills? Do you want to be a comedian or a singer? No matter what your talent may be, it's possible to find fans who will enjoy what you're doing.

Make a Plan

Once you know what to show the world, figure out how you'd like to present it. Having a solid concept can give your projects focus. Although Dawson makes all kinds of videos, he started out as a comedian. His uploads became more and more diverse after he gained experience and followers.

Be Patient

If you don't have thousands of subscribers after your first video, don't worry. Finding an audience can take time. You can make your presence known on social media. Many YouTube stars have large followings on Facebook, Instagram, and Twitter.

Be Consistent

If your uploads have a regular schedule, fans will be more likely to follow your channel. For example, Shane Dawson often records multiple vlogs in a week and releases them one by one. In addition to this, he also spends much of his week planning, writing, filming, and promoting. YouTube stardom can be fun, but success still requires hours of hard work.

had moved away from making offensive content. His new work had become more mature and thoughtful. In his YouTube video "Regarding the rumors about me today," Dawson says, "Back in the day… I loved the feeling of making somebody shocked and laugh because they couldn't believe what was coming out of

Dawson's recent documentaries have been received with critical acclaim and mark a departure from the more juvenile work he did in the past.

my mouth." A week later, he tweeted: "I grew up. I changed my content. I apologized countless times for my…offensive jokes. instead of dragging me down people should use me as an example of a creator who can CHANGE and better themselves and their content. i'm so proud of who i am today."

THE TRUTH ABOUT TANACON

Although YouTube stars are real people, many play more upbeat versions of themselves for their fans. Dawson is a real person, but Shane Dawson at home is not exactly the same as Shane Dawson, YouTube star. Dawson's next three documentary series looked at the real lives of YouTube celebrities.

One of the people Dawson focused on for this interview project is Tana Monceau. Monceau is most famous for her series of Storytime videos on YouTube. She also became famous after being banned from VidCon, a huge yearly gathering of YouTube stars and their fans. After this, Monceau started her own event called TanaCon. In 2018, the convention was cancelled on opening day, and many fans were angry about losing their money. Dawson sat with Monceau as she explained her side of the story. "The Truth About TanaCon" was an enormous success with both fans and the press.

THE SECRET WORLD OF JEFFREE STAR

In August 2018, *The Secret World of Jeffree Star* premiered on shane. Star is a YouTube blogger who became famous as a make-up artist and fashion designer. His successful cosmetic company also helped him reach a net worth of $50 million, according to celebritynetworth.com. Star's career has involved many controversies. In addition to his feuds with Kim Kardashian and Kat Von D, many vloggers and fans have accused him of being mean and racist. Dawson shows viewers Star's extravagant home as well as his business, but also gets Star to reveal some personal details about his past. At the end of the series, both Dawson and viewers have a better understanding of who Star really is and why he behaves as he does.

THE MIND OF JAKE PAUL

Shane Dawson, seen here in Los Angeles on July 15, 2018, is captured in an unguarded moment. When you are famous, cameras appear everywhere.

Another focus of Dawson's documentary series was Jake Paul, a Vine star and cast member on the Disney Channel comedy *Bizaardvark*. By the age of eighteen, Paul had attracted more than five million followers. Off the set, Paul's bad behavior began to cause problems. His dangerous stunts and pranks drew the attention of both his neighbors and the police in Los Angeles. Some of Paul's critics have called him a sociopath. Rather than criticize, Dawson uses the interviews to get a full picture of Jake Paul, bad and good.

The first episode in the eight-part series was uploaded on

September 25, 2008. On that same day, Dawson tweeted, "This series takes a look at Jake's actions over the years and many of those actions involve other people." The series also examined the reasons why people seek fame on YouTube and how fame can change people. Part one received almost ten million views in its first day. Dawson lost some fans who opposed giving publicity and attention to Paul, who has been accused of bullying and verbally abusing women in the past. Others accused Paul of using Dawson to improve his public image. Dawson addressed the accusations. In the same tweet of September 24, 2008, he said: "This month I've learned there's way more than 2 sides to every story. In this case, there was 100." Paul was also apprehensive about allowing Dawson total access to his life. In "Pls Watch This Before Shane Dawson's Series," Paul explains, "I didn't have any influence at all. It's literally completely up to Shane, which is kind of scary." The episodes of *The Mind of Jake Paul* are Dawson's most popular uploads. Considering that he has been posting for ten years, this is quite an achievement.

Today, Shane Dawson is more popular than he ever has been. As his work has become more mature, he has gained new subscribers and followers. Part of Dawson's success has been his ability to change with the times.

His curiosity about the world has also led him to upload videos on a wide variety of subjects. Dawson loves his fans and always wants to release the best content he can. At this point, Dawson doesn't show any signs of stopping doing just that.

TIMELINE

1988 Shane Lee Yaw is born in Long Beach, California.

2006 Shane graduates from Lakewood High School.

2008 Shane Dawson TV debuts on YouTube.

2010 Dawson wins Choice Web Star at the Teen Choice Awards.

2011 Dawson begins dating Lisa Schwartz.

2012 Dawson releases his first single, "SUPERLUV!"

2013 The *Shane and Friends* podcast begins.

2014 Dawson releases *Not Cool.*

2015 Dawson begins his *Mind Blowing Conspiracy Theories* series.

2015 *I Hate Myselfie* is published.

2015 Dawson and Lisa Schwartz end their relationship. He later comes out to his subscribers as bisexual.

2016 Dawson announces his relationship with Ryland Adams.

2016 *It Gets Worse* is published.

June 28, 2018 Dawson uploads the three-episode TanaCon documentary.

August 1, 2018 *The Secret World of Jeffree Starr* debuts.

August 2018 Dawson's YouTube videos reach four billion total views.

September 25, 2018 Part one of *The Mind of Jake Paul* is uploaded to YouTube.

October 2018 Dawson reaches eighteen million YouTube subscribers.

GLOSSARY

accessible Easy to find or understand.

blackface The use of makeup by nonblack performers to make them look like and make fun of African Americans.

blog (short for "web blog") A website used by people to express their personal thoughts and ideas online.

blogosphere The world of all blogs and personal websites on the internet.

body dysmorphic disorder A mental condition that makes people obsess about imaginary physical flaws in an extremely negative way.

controversy An argument over different ideas.

disorder A mental or physical problem.

documentary A film or video that focuses on a real subject or situation.

endorsement Paying a celebrity or influencer to speak positively about a certain product, website, or brand.

influencer A person on social media who can promote ideas or brands to a large audience.

lucrative Making money or wealth.

morbidly obese Being so overweight that a person's overall health is threatened.

parody Books, songs, and films that imitate the style or content of something that is already popular or well known.

racism Believing that a certain race is inferior to yours.

social media Websites or other platforms that connect communities of people online.

sociopath A person who has very little concern for the feelings of others and acts without considering them.

viral Describing videos or blogs that spread across a large segment of the internet very quickly.

vlog (short for "video log") A video blog.

FOR MORE INFORMATION

Alateen

Al-Anon Family Group Head-
quarters, Inc.
1600 Corporate Landing Park-
way
Virginia Beach, VA 23454-5617
(757) 563-1600
Email: who@al-anon.org
Website: https://al-anon.org
Facebook: @AlateenWSO
Twitter: @Alateen_WSO
Alateen is a part of Al-Anon (a
shortened form of Alcoholics
Anonymous) Family Groups.
Al-Anon offers "help and
hope for families and friends
of alcoholics" through books,
workbooks, and group
meetings. The website also
contains links to Al-Anon
programs in Canada.

Anxiety and Depression Asso-
ciation of America (ADAA)

8701 Georgia Avenue, Suite #412
Silver Spring MD 20910
(240) 485-1001
Email: information@adaa.org
Website: https://adaa.org
Facebook: @

AnxietyAndDepressionAsso-
ciationOfAmerica
Twitter: @Got-Anxiety
Instagram: @triumphoveranxiety
ADAA is a nonprofit organiza-
tion that provides information
and support for mental
health disorders, including
depression and body dys-
morphia.

Buffer Festival

2300 Yonge Street, #1600
Toronto, ON M4P 1E4
Canada
(888) 732-1682
Email: support@bufferfestival
.com
Website: https://bufferfestival
.com
Facebook, Twitter, and Instagram: @BufferFestival
The Buffer Festival is an
annual convention that
premiers the latest YouTube
videos. Creators submit videos for one of six categories,
and winners are honored at
an awards show.

Center for Media Literacy (CML)

22603 Pacific Coast Highway, #549
Malibu, CA 90265
(310) 804-3985
Email: cml@medialit.com
Website: http://www.medialit.org
Facebook: @Center-for
-Media-Literacy
CML was formed to help people live and learn in a global media culture.

FAN EXPO Canada

20 Eglinton Avenue W
Suite 1200
PO Box 2055
Toronto ON M4R 1K8
Canada
(416) 960-9030
Email: info@fanexpohq.com
Website: http://www
.fanexpocanada.com
Facebook and Twitter:
@fanexpocanada
Instagram: @officialfxc
FAN EXPO is the third-largest pop culture event in North America and an annual science fiction convention that attracts gamers, artists, and YouTube celebrities.

The Streamys

Dick Clark Productions, Inc.
2900 Olympic Boulevard
Santa Monica, CA 90404
(310) 255-4600
Email: support@streamys.org
Website: https://streamys.org
Facebook, Twitter, and Instagram: @streamys
The Streamys are held once a year in Beverly Hills, CA. Awards are given in more than forty categories at what *Vanity Fair* magazine calls the "Oscars of the Web."

VidCon

PO Box 8147
Missoula, MT
(406) 207-6999
Email: info@vidcon.com
Website: http://vidcon.com
Facebook and Twitter: @VidCon
VidCon is the largest convention celebrating online videos and their creators in the world. The company has been hosting annual events since 2009 in the United States, England, and Australia.

FOR FURTHER READING

Albers, Susan. *Eating Mindfully for Teens: A Workbook to Help You Make Healthy Choices, End Emotional Eating, and Feel Great.* Oakland, CA: New Harbinger, 2018.

Birley, Shane. *How to Be a Blogger and Vlogger in 10 Easy Lessons: Learn How to Create Your Own Blog, Vlog, or Podcast and Get It Out in the Blogosphere!* (Super Skills). Lake Forest, CA: Walter Foster Jr., 2016.

Blomfield, Robert. *How to Make a Movie in 10 Easy Lessons: Learn How to Write, Direct, ad Edit Your Own Film Without a Hollywood Budget* (Super Skills). Lake Forest, CA: Walter Foster Jr., 2015.

Ciampa, Rob, and Theresa Moore. *YouTube Channels For Dummies.* Hoboken, NJ: John Wiley & Sons, 2015.

Dawson, Shane. *I Hate Myselfie: A Collection of Essays.* New York, NY: Atria/Keywords Press, 2015.

Dawson, Shane. *It Gets Worse: A Collection of Essays.* New York, NY: Atria/Keywords Press, 2016.

Kenney, Karen. *Make and Upload Your Own Videos.* Minneapolis, MN: Lerner Publishing Company, 2018.

Meyer, Terry Teague. *I Have an Alcoholic Parent. Now What?* (Teen Life 411). New York, NY: Rosen Young Adult, 2015.

Schroeppel, Tom, and Chuck DeLaney. *The Bare Bones Camera Course for Film and Video.* New York, NY: Allworth Press, 2015.

White, Oli. *Generation Next.* London, UK: Quercus, 2016.

Willoughby, Nick. *Digital Filmmaking for Kids.* Hoboken, NJ: John Wiley & Sons, 2015.

Willoughby, Nick. *Making YouTube Videos.* Hoboken, NJ: John Wiley & Sons, 2015.

BIBLIOGRAPHY

Alexander, Julia. "Shane Dawson's New Documentaries Crack YouTube Culture's Kardashian Problem." Polygon, August 3, 2018. https://www.polygon.com/2018/8/3/17642862 /shane-dawson-jeffree-star-documentary-keeping-up -kardashians.

Bradley, Laura. "Why Disney Just Severed Ties with a Famously Obnoxious YouTuber." *Vanity Fair*, July 25, 2017. https://www .vanityfair.com/hollywood/2017/07/jake-paul-disney-bizaard vark-neighbors-controversy.

Celebrity Net Worth. "Jeffree Star Net Worth." Celebrity Net Worth. Retrieved September 4, 2018. https://www.celebritynetworth .com/richest-celebrities/models/jeffree-star-net-worth.

Considine, Austin. "Shane Dawson, YouTube's Comic for the Under-30 Set." *New York Times*, April 2, 2010. https://www .nytimes.com/2010/04/04/fashion/04youtube.html.

Dachille, Arielle. "YouTube Star Shane Dawson Apologizes for Racist Videos & I'm Not Buying It." Bustle, April 25, 2018, www.bustle.com/articles/41633-youtube-star-shane-dawson -apologizes-for-racist-videos-im-not-buying-it-video.

Dawson, Shane. *Confronting My Dad.* YouTube, November 29, 2017. https://www.youtube.com/watch?v =LU6xDgpnIyM.

Dawson, Shane. *CONFRONTING MY FIRST LOVE.* YouTube, October 18, 2017. https://www.youtube.com /watch?v=_95NxbsbMF4.

Dawson, Shane. *Flaws.* YouTube, November 4, 2008. https:// www.youtube.com/watch?v=a8Cd4iG73ak.

Dawson, Shane. *FORMER FATTY.* YouTube, September 12, 2008. https://shanedawson.livejournal.com/1523.html.

Dawson, Shane. *FRED IS DEAD!* YouTube, September 12, 2008. https://www.youtube.com/watch?v=_NLXIZivlyA.

Dawson, Shane. *HAUNTED HOUSE PARTY!!! *INTERACTIVE GAME* (START HERE).* YouTube, October 30, 2010. https://www.youtube.com/watch?v=gwi21aKySWY.

Dawson, Shane. *Hodini's Street Magic.* YouTube, February 13, 2010. https://www.youtube.com/watch?v=EXdXJP0iZTM.

Dawson, Shane. *I Hate Myselfie.* New York, NY: Atria/Keywords Press, 2015.

Dawson, Shane. *It Gets Worse: A Collection of Essays.* New York, NY: Atria/Keywords Press, 2016.

Dawson, Shane. *The Mind of Jake Paul.* YouTube, September 25, 2018. https://www.youtube.com/watch?time_continue =2&v=9bpkr91p2xY.

Dawson, Shane. *My Apology (Blackface & Offensive Videos).* YouTube, September 25, 2014. https://www.youtube.com /watch?v=3jZDt5zQWsE.

Dawson, Shane. *My Eating Disorder.* YouTube, October 1, 2018. https://www.youtube.com/watch?v=EPSxheNL2yk.

Dawson, Shane. *Regarding the rumors about me today.* YouTube, January 10, 2018. https://www.youtube.com /watch?v=I7B0z_2EZmQ.

Dawson, Shane. *Sarah Palin Music Video.* YouTube, October 5, 2008. https://www.youtube.com/watch?v=f6MjGUHfWmY.

Dawson, Shane. *The Secret World of Jeffree Star.* YouTube, August 1, 2018. https://www.youtube.com/watch?v =xUf2-sjGqQw&list=PLaGL4End-91BhoJF0jwE4D8 -1D4M7bl9L.

Dawson, Shane. *Shane Dawson's 'Love Story.'* YouTube, December 18, 2010. https://www.youtube.com/watch?v =Dk2xsRpaJoo.

Dawson, Shane. *The Truth About Tanacon.* YouTube, June 28, 2018. https://www.youtube.com/watch?v=8xFtIsyRvNE.

Dawson, Shane. *YOUTUBE GOT ME FIRED!* YouTube, August 29, 2008. https://www.youtube.com/watch?v=Jdlqc5WCqSs.

Ewalt, David M. "The Web Celeb 25." *Forbes*, February 2, 2010. http://www.forbes.com/2010/02/02/web-celebrities -internet-thought-leaders-2010.html.

Farokhmanesh, Megan. "Shane Dawson's New Docuseries Asks: Is Jake Paul a Sociopath?" The Verge, September 25, 2018. https://www.theverge.com/2018/9/25/17902020 /shane-dawson-jake-paul-docuseries-first-episode.

Feldman, Kate. "YouTube Star Shane Dawson Apologizes for Jokes about Pedophilia." *NY Daily News*, January 10, 2018. http://www.nydailynews.com/entertainment /youtube-star-shane-dawson-apologizes-jokes-pedophilia -article-1.3750545.

Frankel, Todd C. "Why Almost No One Is Making a Living on YouTube." *Washington Post*, March 2, 2018. https:// www.washingtonpost.com/news/the-switch/wp /2018/03/02/why-almost-no-one-is-making-a-living -on-youtube/?noredirect=on&utm_term=.c3aaaf1f5efd.

Guzman, Richard. "Long Beach native Shane Dawson talks winning 'The Chair' and his harsh critics." *Long Beach Press-Telegram,* November 12, 2014. https://www .presstelegram.com/2014/11/12/long-beach-native -shane-dawson-talks-winning-the-chair-and-his-harsh -critics/.

Heavy.com. "Shane Dawson Net Worth: 5 Fast Facts You Need to Know." August 7, 2018. https://heavy.com/news/2018/08 /shane-dawson-net-worth.

Miller, Liz Shannon. "YouTube Elite Make Old Tricks Work For The Station." Gigaom, August 20, 2009. http://gigaom .com/2009/08/20/youtube-elite-make-old-tricks-work-for -the-station.

O'Neill, Megan. "Shane Dawson & The Fine Brothers on

YouTube Collaboration & Shane's Christmas Special."
Adweek, December 21, 2010, https://www.adweek.com
/digital/shane-dawson-christmas.

Paul, Jake. "Pls Watch This Before Shane Dawson's Series…"
YouTube, September 25, 2018. https://www.youtube.com
/watch?v=ERVmfE-GISk.

Rexrode, Martina. "Shane Dawson Continues to Give a Platform to
Racists and Violent Teenagers." *Arts + Culture*, September 25,
2017. http://culture.affinitymagazine.us/shane-dawson
-continues-to-give-a-platform-to-racists-and-violent-teenagers.

Romano, Aja. "Racist Blackface 'Comedy' Is Making a Come-
back—on YouTube." *Washington Post*, September 30, 2014.
http://www.washingtonpost.com/news/the-intersect
/wp/2014/09/30/racist-blackface-comedy-is-making-a
-comeback-on-youtube/?noredirect=on&utm_term
=.a9ec57537844.

Roth, Madeline. "YouTube Star Shane Dawson Comes Out as
Bisexual: 'I Am Open To Love'." MTV News, July 9, 2015.
http://www.mtv.com/news/2207848/shane-dawson-comes
-out-as-bisexual.

@shanedawson. "a note about the mind of jakepaul." Twitter,
January 10, 2018, 2:27 p.m. https://twitter.com/shanedawson
/status/1044658873464848384.

@shanedawson. "I grew up. I changed my content. I apologized
countless times for my s****y offensive jokes. instead of
dragging me down people should use me as an example
of a creator who can CHANGE and better themselves and
their content. i'm so proud of who i am today." Twitter, January
10, 2018, 2:27 p.m. https://twitter.com/shanedawson/status
/951218847972917248

shanedawsonforever. "Shane Dawson FIRST EVER VIDEO! (The
411)." YouTube, December 11, 2011. https://www.youtube
.com/watch?v=YcA9svlHuT4.

ShaneDawsonLIVE. "Shane Dawson Plays 'Quick Question Answers: Day One: Round Two' on Shane Dawson's BlogTv." YouTube, March 4, 2009. https://www.youtube.com /watch?v=B7X30jG1Ndw.

STATION, The, by Maker. *ZOMBIES TAKE OVER YOUTUBE!!!!!!* YouTube, August 8, 2009. https://www.youtube.com/watch ?v=czWoP7qVNSI.

Ward, Tom. "All Aboard the Shane Train: An Interview with Shane Dawson." *Forbes*, July 27, 2017. https://www.forbes.com /sites/tomward/2017/07/27/all-aboard-the-shane-train-an -interview-with-shane-dawson.

INDEX

ABOUT THE AUTHOR

Kerry Hinton has never posted a video to YouTube, but he considers himself a fan of the site's archival capabilities. Most of his favorite channels feature commercials, movie trailers, and television shows from the 1960s, '70s, and '80s. Channels featuring music videos from those eras run a close second. He lives in Brooklyn, New York, with his cat, Chicken.

PHOTO CREDITS

Design and Layout: Michael Moy; Editor: Xina M. Uhl; Photo Researcher: Nicole DiMella